Cousins

If you're lucky,
a cousin is there
from the beginning.

A cousin can be
a girl or boy and as
close to you as a sister
or brother.

A cousin is
the child of your
mommy or daddy's
brother or sister.

So, you're really lucky because you get an uncle and aunt too.

A cousin shares
a grandmother and
grandfather with you, so there
is even more love
to go around.

A cousin can join you on family adventures.

A cousin will
eat with you at
the kids' table,

making lifelong
memories of family
get-togethers
and holidays.

A cousin may not always agree with you,

but that's
what makes life
interesting.

A cousin can
help you learn, by
sharing their talents
and encouraging
yours.

A cousin is loyal
and there when you
need help.

A cousin
will tell you
the truth.

A cousin
can keep your
secrets.

A cousin will understand when you cry.

A cousin
will take care
of you.

A cousin can
make you laugh
and enjoy the
good times.

A cousin will
want their friends to
be your friends.

A cousin can be
your best childhood
playmate, who grows
up to be your forever
friend.

This book is dedicated to my son, Jordan Bolch, who shared with me his love of family and endless creativity, together with his tireless effort and generous commitment of time, to make it a reality.

ABOUT THE AUTHOR

Susan Bolch is a native of Philadelphia, Pennsylvania, who has a passion for words. She is a graduate of Barnard College of Columbia University and Georgetown University Law Center. She is the author of a novel, "The Cufflink". Susan lives in Naples, Florida and can be reached at susanbolch@gmail.com.

Executive Producer Jordan Bass Bolch
Editor in Chief Richie Schwab
Illustrator Aquarellina
Plusia Publishing © 2017

For more information visit
plusiapublishing.com

Printed in U.S.A.

For more information visit
plusiapublishing.com